ASIAN PRESENCE in EUROPE

by Zerbanoo Gifford

MANTRA

Acknowledgements
The Author and the Publishers would like to thank the following:
Professor Banatvala, Sudha Bhuchar, Anup Biswas, Carla Contractor, Zane Dalal,
Robin Dutt, Byram Jeejeebhoy, Farrokh Kavarana, Zubin Mehta,
Yusuf Hamied & Cynthia Meister, Dhruva Mistry, Kumar Rupesinghe &
David Reed of International Alert, Sehri Saklatvala, Ravi & Sukanya Shankar,
Darshan Singh Bhuller, Professor Richard Sorabji, Meera Syal,
the late JRD Tata, Naseem Khan, Kusoom Vadgama, Jatinder Verma,
Rozina Visram and Neville Wadia.

Picture Sources
By permission of The British Library: 9 - WD 1288;
Kew Photographics: 12; The Wadia Family: 14 & 16; JRD Tata: 17;
Zoroastrian Trust Funds of Europe: 20; Sehri Saklatvala: 22;
Somerville College, Oxford: 30; Indian High Commission: 32;
Hulton Deutsch Collection Ltd: 41 & 44; Stephen J Line: 42;
By courtesy of The National Portrait Gallery, London: 46;
Hugo Glendinning: 48, 49 & 53; Peter Gordon-Stables: 51;
Trupti Tate & Birmingham City Council: 52;
John Tyrell: 66

Designed by Jyoti Bhikha

Published by
Mantra Publishing Ltd
5 Alexandra Grove
London N12 8NU

*For my parents,
who taught me the joys of my remarkable heritage,
and to fight for what is right and good in life.*

Zerbanoo Gifford's royalties are given to Anti-Slavery International's work to help end child bonded labour.

Anti-Slavery International, the world's oldest human rights group, is currently working with local organisations in South Asia to end the practice of bonded labour particularly of children. Many children are forced to work in poor conditions and without pay in return for debts incurred by their parents.

Anti-Slavery International
The Stableyard, Broomgrove Road
London SW9 9TL.

INTRODUCTION

Even before 1832, when the first Indian ambassador, Rammohun Roy, arrived in Britain, Asians have been making their mark in Europe. Many of them are unknown today, and Asian Presence in Europe is an attempt to correct their omission from our histories. Within these pages is a personal selection of remarkable men and women, some of the Asian heroes and heroines of Europe's forgotten history.

I hope to make the lives and deeds of those included more accessible, particularly to younger people, whatever their own cultural heritage. Today, more than ever, we all need to be inspired by those who dedicated themselves to a central vision, of making the world a better place.

Struggles against injustice are all interconnected, and many of the people in this book recognised this. The breadth of their vision takes in women's rights, racial equality and the right to self-government. They have excelled in many fields, from music, literature and the arts to science, politics, law and business. The short stories in this book cannot do justice to their achievements, and I have had to leave out enough material to fill several volumes. Even in this short format, their stories show the importance of courage and commitment in overcoming the barriers of prejudice, which are still preventing people from realising their full potential.

One can only admire radicals like Dadabhai Naoroji, Britain's first Asian Member of Parliament, who won the hearts of the suffragettes with his support for women's rights. They can all inspire us in different ways.

The women who have been included have had to overcome entrenched prejudice, and have done so with fiery determination that makes the stories of their lives even more compelling. Some. like Cornelia Sorabji, notched up so many firsts, that one can only marvel at their dedication.

The women are my personal favourites, particularly the beautiful and complex Noor-un-nisa Inayat Khan, GC , the war heroine and British spy. Her story is perhaps the most fascinating of all.

I would like to thank the many people who have contributed to this project especially Lisa Barry, John Tyrell and Ian Watters and to Mantra for recognising the importance of publishing such books for young people.

Finally, I am happy to dedicate the proceeds of this book to Anti-Slavery International to help with their work relieving the suffering of millions of children in bonded labour worldwide.

CONTENTS

Raja Rammohun Roy 9
Sir Jamsetji Jeejeebhoy 12
The Wadia Family 14
JRD Tata 17
Dadabhai Naoroji 20
Shapurji Saklatvala 22
Bhikhaji Cama 25
Sir Jagadish Chandra Bose 28
Cornelia Sorabji 30
Krishna Menon 32
Dr Kumar Rupesinghe 34
Noor-un-nisa Inayat Khan 36
Professor J E Banatvala 40

Prince Ranjitsinhji 41
Jahangir Khan 42

Rabindranath Tagore 44
Uday Shankar 46
Shobana Jeyasingh 48
Darshan Singh Bhuller 49
Robin Dutt 51
Dhruva Mistry 52
Jatinder Verma 53
Sudha Bhuchar 55
Meera Syal 56

Ravi Shankar 57
Zubin Mehta 59
Zane Dalal 61
Anup Biswas 63
Freddie Mercury 64
Apache Indian 66

Glossary 68

Raja Rammohun Roy

Rammohun Roy became known as the *"father of modern India"* for his achievements in the areas of education, women's rights and religious reform. He came to Britain, as the first Indian ambassador, more than one hundred and sixty years ago.

Born in Bengal, India, in 1772, Rammohun Roy worked for the East India Company before leaving to become a successful businessman. He also wrote many books, including the first Bengali dictionary and grammar, and religious works. When he was stopped from using a printing press which was owned by Europeans, he started his own. Roy produced two newspapers, one in Bengali, one in Persian, with a mixture of news, articles and comment.

Believing that education, especially science, would be the key to bring about Indian unity and prosperity, Rammohun Roy co-founded Calcutta's Presidency College. His textbooks on grammar, geography and geometry were given out free of charge so that as many people as possible could learn from them.

A Hindu Brahmin, Rammohun Roy upset many of his contemporaries, including his mother, by trying to stop old customs such as child marraige, idol worship and particularly sati (the burning to death of a widow on her husband's funeral pyre). This may have been because he was so shocked when he saw his sister-in-law jump onto the fire at his brother's funeral. Sometimes women were murdered if they did not kill themselves. Rammohun Roy felt strongly that such cruelty needed to be opposed by both men and women.

Rammohun Roy was an expert in other religions too, including Buddhism and Islam. Wanting to read the Christian Bible in its original languages, he learnt

Hebrew, Greek and Latin. He believed in religious tolerance, and thought there was just one *"author and preserver of the Universe"*, an *"Eternal Being"* known by different names. Rammohun Roy started the Brahmo Samaj, or Believer's Society, to encourage worship across religions.

Akbar Shah II, the Mogul Emperor of India, gave Rammohun Roy the title 'Rajah', (ruler), and asked him to go to Britain to represent him in a dispute with the East India Company over the confiscation of his land. Rammohun Roy arrived in Liverpool, England, on 8th April 1831, with his adopted son, his cook, a gardener who had asked to see England and two cows!

As ambassador, Rammohun Roy met Britain's new king, William IV, and was invited to his coronation in Westminster Abbey. Later he advised Parliament on Indian affairs. India's highest court and law-making body at that time was the British Privy Council, a government body that advised the monarch in London. The British had made sati illegal in 1829, but some Hindu priests wanted to keep the practice. Rammohun Roy spoke to the Privy Council and made sure that this did not happen.

He travelled around Britain, creating great interest wherever he went. At one Manchester factory, the police were needed to control the crowds. Rammohun Roy spoke to the crowd in favour of the Great Reform Act of 1832 which gave the vote to many more men in Britain. One English woman who met him wrote, *"Scarcely any description can do justice to his admirable qualities, and the charm of his society, his extended knowledge, his comprehension of mind, his universal philanthropy, his genuine dignity mixed with perfect courtesy, and the most touching humility. His memory I shall cherish on many accounts, but the character in which I best love to contemplate him is that of the friend and champion of women."*

Rammohun Roy supported the Irish people's struggle against absentee landlords and always took a great interest in freedom around the world. In Calcutta in 1823, Rammohun Roy gave a great public dinner on hearing that a democratic government had been set up in Spain, saying, *"Ought I to be insensible to the sufferings of my fellow creatures wherever they are, or however unconnected by interests, religion or language?"*

Rammohun Roy also visited France where he dined with King Louis Philippe, the last king of France. He

had to get a visa and he wrote a long letter to the French Foreign Minister complaining about such restrictions on peaceful travels. It is interesting that such barriers are only now ending in Europe for EC citizens.

In September 1833, Rammohun Roy visited Bristol to see a friend, the leading Unitarian minister, Lant Carpenter. He spoke from the pulpit of Carpenter's chapel to an *"overflowing congregation"*. A few days afterwards, Roy fell ill and was told he was suffering from 'brain fever', now known as meningitis. He died ten days later.

Rammohun Roy was buried in the large gardens of the Bristol home in which he was staying, *"in silence and without ceremony"*, as he had requested. Some years later, the house was sold and Rammohun Roy's body was re-buried under a beautiful monument at Arno's Vale Cemetery, Bristol. It was paid for by a friend, Dwarkanath Tagore, the grandfather of the winner of the Nobel Prize for Literature, Rabindranath Tagore.

People still visit the monument of Raja Rammohun Roy to revere the memory of the *"father of modern India"*, a truly remarkable and enlightened man.

The tomb of Raja Rammohun Roy at Bristol

Sir Jamsetji Jeejeebhoy

Byram Jeejeebhoy with statue of his ancestor, Sir Jamsetji

Starting life as a bottle-washer, Sir Jamsetji Jeejeebhoy rose to be one of the world's richest men, establishing a trading empire. An extraordinary philanthropist, he gave away almost two-thirds of his immense wealth during his lifetime.

Born in Bombay, India, in 1783, he was only five when his family moved to Navsari in Western India. At sixteen he was orphaned and, with a small gift of food from a neighbour, walked to Bombay in search of work.

There, Jamsetji Jeejeebhoy worked in his uncle's bottle business. Later, a cousin was trading between China and India and hired him as a cashier. He then went into the China trade himself, taking cotton and opium to China, returning with silks and other goods.

During the Napoleonic Wars, French warships were sent to disrupt trade to and from British India. Jamsetji Jeejeebhoy had just married his cousin when, in 1807, he was captured by the French. They took

his cargo as booty, and Jamsetji Jeejeebhoy and the other passengers as prisoners, to what is now South Africa, then a Dutch possession. During this time he became friends with the ship's surgeon, William Jardine, who later helped found Jardine Matheson, the international trading company.

During Jamsetji Jeejeebhoy's captivity, his father-in-law kept the business going. Trading continued, and by the time of Jamsetji Jeejeebhoy's release, he was a rich man. The business continued to grow, with Jamsetji Jeejeebhoy owning a fleet of ships and chartering others, trading between India, China, Siam (now Thailand), Italy and England.

Jamsetji Jeejeebhoy now started to use his wealth to help others and in 1822, the year of his eldest son's marriage, he freed all the men in a

debtor's prison by paying their debts.

In 1837, a fire in Surat, on the coast of Gujarat, India, destroyed twenty thousand homes. Jamsetji Jeejeebhoy immediately sent a ship to the stricken city with a cargo of food, clothing and money. He paid for the building of many public water systems, Bombay's first hospitals, the famous Sir Jamsetji Jeejeebhoy School of Art and even started an animal sanctuary.

In 1850 Jamsetji Jeejeebhoy visited Navsari, where the local prince ordered that drums be beaten continuously in his honour during the time he was there. Although initially flattered, Jamsetji Jeejeebhoy, soon had to send a messenger to the prince asking for the drummers to stop so that everyone could get some sleep! Before he left he found the woman who, in 1799, had given him food for his journey to Bombay, and rewarded her a thousand times over for her gift.

In 1827, he was the first Indian juror and in 1834 he became the first Indian magistrate. He also started one of the first Indian-owned newspapers.

Jamsetji Jeejeebhoy's good works

extended to Europe. He sent large sums of money to Ireland in 1822 and 1846, when the population faced starvation. He also sent money to France in 1856 when there was severe flooding.

He was an unusual man for his time, a supporter of female education and emancipation and, by introducing his wife and daughters to society, outraged many more traditional Indians who thought that women should not be seen in public.

In 1841, he became Sir Jamsetji then, in 1855, was given the Freedom of the City of London, receiving the honour in the same year as the famous explorer and missionary, David Livingstone. In 1877, Sir Jamsetji Jeejeebhoy was made the first Indian Baronet, a hereditary knight. Two years later he died in Bombay.

It is often said of famous people that *"their name will live forever"* and in Jamsetji Jeejeebhoy's case this is true. Not only must each holder of the title give up his own name and become known as the new Sir Jamsetji Jeejeebhoy, but even today his Zoroastrian Parsi Benevolent Institution continues working in his name.

The Wadia Family

Lowjee Nusserwanjee founded a dynasty of master shipbuilders and modern industrialists - the Wadia family. His achievements in the eighteenth century highlight an Indian technical mastery that was ahead of its Western counterparts.

By 1736 Surat had been a ship-building centre for centuries. At a time when the average British ship could hold around 350 tons of cargo, Surat shipyards had built many ships of 1,200 tons.

In the same year, the East India Company in Bombay wrote a letter to its counterpart in Surat, saying that they needed a good shipbuilding carpenter and *"we are told that there is one in Surat named Lowjee. If he will come hither he shall have all fitting encouragement."*
The young man in question went to Bombay. The company complained at his price and wrote that they *"hoped they would deserve it by their performance"*. They need not have worried. With his team of ten carpenters, Lowjee Nusserwanjee

Neville and Nusli Wadia

transformed shipbuilding and repair in the town.

The dry dock Lowjee Nusserwanjee built at Bombay was the first in India and is still in use today. The East India Company was delighted at the dock's success and no longer thought that Lowjee Nusserwanjee was too expensive. Instead, they gave him presents to thank him.

By the time of his death in 1774, the family had taken the surname 'Wadia', which means 'ship-builder'. Two of his sons took over the business and their work was also highly thought of.

The rise in sea trade meant that English shipbuilders were running short of supplies of wood. English oak, the traditional wood used to build British ships, was scarce

because the English forests were being cut down faster than new trees could grow and mature. So the Wadias were asked to build ships in Bombay using Indian Malabar teak. Many thought the Indian ships would be badly made, too heavy and would soon rot when they were put into seawater. In fact, the Wadia ships were not only cheaper, they were easier to sail and proved to last an average of thirty years compared to the twelve years of oak ships. Some lasted much longer, such as the *Swallow*, which was launched in 1777 and was finally sunk in 1823.

The British navy started to buy their ships from the East India Company. The first ship was the frigate, *Cornwallis*. Hidden away under the deck was some writing: *"This ship was built by a damned black fellow, AD 1800"*. It had been carved by Jamsetjee Bomanjee Wadia as a protest against the prejudiced attitudes shown by some British owners of the family's ships.

Another Wadia ship ordered by the Royal Navy was named *HMS Cornwallis* after the earlier frigate which had been lost. Launched in 1813, two wars were ended on its decks. In 1815 it defeated an American sloop in the last action of the War of 1812 between Great Britain and the USA. In 1842 the

Treaty of Nanking was signed on board, ending a war with China. *Cornwallis* was then converted into a steamship and was sent to fight in the Baltic Sea. It ended its days as part of the jetty at Sheerness, Kent in the 1860s. Finally broken up in 1957, the hull was discovered to be still seaworthy over 140 years after its launch.

The world's oldest active sailing ship is Wadia-built. The training ship, *Foudroyant*, started its life in Bombay as *HMS Trincomalee* in 1817.

The Wadia family used their shipbuilding fortune to start several new businesses. They were famed for having the first home in Bombay lit by gas which attracted great crowds. The family's interest in the latest technology continued when they helped launch India Radio and Communication Company which linked India and Britain by radio for the first time in the 1920s.

Among the most successful of their new enterprises was their work with the Bombay Dyeing and Manufacturing Company, started in 1879. India was the world's largest producer of cotton, yet most Indians then wore clothes that were dyed by hand, or dyed in factories in Britain. The Indian mills were running short of cloth because of import

restrictions, so Nowrosjee Wadia asked a millowner, Sir Dinshaw Petit, to start a partnership to produce more cloth. The company grew until it needed to develop its own mills to produce cloth to dye. Today the company's main mill in Bombay is Asia's largest textile business under one roof.

After Nowrosjee's death, the company was run by his sons, Cusrow, Ness and Rustom. Today, the company's Honorary President is Neville Wadia, son of Sir Ness Wadia. Born in Liverpool in 1911, he studied at Cambridge University and joined the family dyeing firm in 1931. In 1938, he married Dina Jinnah, daughter of Muhammed Ali Jinnah, the founder of Pakistan. Neville became a director of his family's company, and chairman after his father's death in 1952.

His only son, Nusli, took over the business on Neville's retirement in 1977. In turn, when Nusli retires, his two sons, Ness and Jeh, will do the same. The dynasty founded on industry and established by Lowji Nusserwanji in the eighteenth century still continues today.

The signing and sealing of the Treaty of Nanking which gave Hong Kong to the British, on board HMS Cornwallis.

The British Empire was founded on sea trade. It provided raw materials and new markets for British goods, and the bigger Wadia ships meant higher profits for each voyage. The Wadia ships also suited the Royal Navy, which needed strong reliable ships for its crucial role in policing the Empire.

JRD Tata

A little boy stood on a French beach watching the aviator, Louis Blériot. Years later he too became an aviation pioneer, founding Air India. Throughout India he became known simply by his initials - JRD.

JRD's father was a Zoroastrian Parsi who married a Frenchwoman. She took the name 'Sooni' and, for many years they lived in France. Jehangir Ratanji Dadabhai Tata, the second of their five children, was born in Paris in 1904. He grew up in a bilingual household, speaking English and French. When he was five, the family moved to the French coast of the English Channel. Their new neighbour, Louis Blériot, had just made the first flight across the English Channel in 1909, and used to land his plane on the beach. JRD was spellbound by the magic of flight for the rest of his life.

When the First World War began in 1914, JRD wanted to join the French Air Force but was too young and, in any case, his father's business took the family to India and Japan. They returned to France in 1919 where his mother, Sooni, died of tuberculosis at the age of forty-three.

Like all French men, JRD had to serve for one year in the French Army, which he enjoyed so much that he wanted to stay on to become an officer. His father was totally against the idea and ordered JRD back to Bombay. It turned out to be a fortunate decision for JRD because shortly afterwards all the men in his army unit were killed by rebels in Morocco.

JRD joined the family business in 1925, becoming a director of Tata Sons after a year, following the death of his father. In 1929 JRD, realising he would spend the rest of his life in India, gave up his French citizenship.

The same year he qualified as a pilot, the first person in India to do

so. His licence was marked 'Licence Number 1'. Another flying enthusiast, the Aga Khan, offered a prize of £500 for the first Indian to fly from India to England, or from England to India. JRD nearly won but was beaten by a friend, Aspy Engineer. Aspy's win was made possible because of JRD's generosity in giving him fresh spark plugs when they both landed in Alexandria, Egypt. Aspy was later to become Air Chief Marshal of the Indian Air Force and an Indian Ambassador.

JRD persuaded the Tatas to start an airmail service within India, with JRD flying the plane on some of the routes. It became very successful and JRD was made chairman of the Tata Group. He still had to convince people that passenger flights would also be a success.

JRD thought seriously about becoming a politician as he wanted to see the end of British rule in India. Many Indian leaders were being put in prison by the British at that time and JRD said, *"I realised there was something more useful I could do for my country than go to jail"*. He knew that having flourishing Indian-owned industries would be vital for India when it had won its freedom.

After Independence, Air India began flying to destinations outside India and became known as Air India International. JRD always took a great interest in his airline and the staff had to be prepared to respond to his written comments after all his flights. One famous suggestion was that the overhead lights should be switched on when serving meals as it made the cutlery sparkle more! Even when the airline was taken over by the Indian government he stayed as chairman until 1977.

Although he retired as chairman of Tata Sons in 1991, JRD's influence in the multinational company lived on. He had enjoyed running his own airline business and allowed the leaders of the Tatas' other industries - including steel, chemicals, textiles, electronics and hotels - a great deal of freedom themselves. *"Get the best people and set them free"*, was his advice to other leaders.

Although JRD had earlier turned down a British knighthood, in 1992 he accepted the Bharat Ratna, India's highest civilian award. The same year he was given the United Nations Population Award for his commitment to family planning. Like many others concerned with social justice, JRD was dedicated to enhancing the role of women in society through education.

One story is typical of JRD's modesty and kindness. On seeing two women stranded by their broken-down car, JRD stopped and restarted their car. Only after he had wished them well and departed did the two ladies realise that their car mechanic had been the legendary JRD Tata.

JRD died in December 1993 in Geneva, Switzerland, after a heart attack, and is buried near his birthplace in Paris. To honour his memory, Bombay Airport was renamed JRD Tata International Airport in 1994.

Dadabhai Naoroji

Dadabhai Naoroji was a remarkable man who dedicated his life to political, social and economic reform in both Britain and India. Known as the Grand Old Man of India, he became Britain's first Asian Member of Parliament, elected in 1892.

Dadabhai Naoroji was born near Bombay in 1825 to a poor Zoroastrian Parsi family. His father died soon afterwards, leaving his mother to bring him up alone. Thanks to a scholarship from his community, Dadabhai Naoroji was able to study and became the first Indian Professor of Mathematics. He spent the rest of his life repaying the debt, to the benefit of the whole of India. He started by using his teaching skills to open schools for girls and launched a newspaper to help change public opinion in the need for women's equality.

In 1855, Dadabhai Naoroji made the first of his many journeys to Britain as a partner in the first Indian-owned company there.

In those days India was ruled from Britain and India had no say in its own government. Dadabhai Naoroji wanted to find out the real cost of British rule. It was clear to everyone that while Britain was getting richer, India was becoming poorer. Thanks to him, it was shown that much of Britain's army and navy was paid for by India, even if they did not help defend India. As a result, India was forced to pay heavy and unfair taxes.

Back in India, Dadabhai Naoroji helped found the Indian National Congress. This was a group of influential Indians who met each year to discuss the future of India. It became the leading group campaigning for changes in British rule and, later, in the fight for Indian Independence.

In 1886 Dadabhai Naoroji returned to Britain, determined to become an

MP so he could speak for the millions of people in India who were denied a voice in the Parliament that ruled them. The Conservative Prime Minister of the day, Lord Salisbury, thought he would never succeed. He said, *"I doubt if we have yet got to that point of view where a British constituency would elect a blackman."* The speech outraged many people and Queen Victoria reprimanded Lord Salisbury.

After many difficulties Dadabhai Naoroji stood as the Liberal candidate for the London seat of Finsbury Central. He was helped by Mahatma Gandhi, Muhammed Ali Jinnah, (later to become the founder of Pakistan), Florence Nightingale, Josephine Butler (a leading suffragette), and Keir Hardy, (who later became the first Labour MP). He won by just five votes, earning him the nickname of 'Mr Narrow-Majority'.

The news of his historic victory quickly reached India where people were overjoyed. Not everyone was so enthusiastic, and a few were openly racist. A London newspaper, *The Stephen's Review*, referred to the sacred fire that burns in Zoroastrian temples when it wrote: *"Central Finsbury should be ashamed of itself at having publicly confessed that there was not…an Englishman, a Scotsman, a Welshman or an Irishman as worthy of their votes as this fire-worshipper from Bombay."*

In the next election in 1895, there was a swing against the Liberal Party. Dadabhai Naoroji was one of the many Liberals who were defeated.

In 1904, at the age of seventy-four, after years of dedication to improving the lives of the millions of Indians through the Parliamentary system, Dadabhai Naoroji finally decided to become more radical. He became the first leading figure to call for 'swaraj' or 'independence' for India.

Ill health forced him to retire to India in 1907 and Dadabhai Naoroji died peacefully in 1917, aged ninety-one. His dream of an independent India would take thirty more years to achieve but Dadabhai Naoroji had, in Gandhi's words, *"acted like a father"* to the generation that would achieve it.

Shapurji Saklatvala

Comrade Saks with his wife in Paris.

Shapurji Saklatvala was known as Comrade Saks, a fiery fighter against prejudice and injustice. He was elected Britain's third Asian Member of Parliament in 1922.

Shapurji Saklatvala was born in Bombay in 1874. After his father's death, he was brought up by his uncle, the industrialist, JN Tata.

There was an outbreak of the plague in Bombay between 1896 and 1902. Many people died because there was no vaccine to protect against the disease, so a famous Russian doctor was asked to help. Shapurji Saklatvala was to be his assistant, and went to the European Club, (where the doctor was staying), but was refused entry because he was Indian. After much argument, he was let in through the kitchen, and the two men met in a small basement. The insulting treatment Shapurji Saklatvala had received reinforced his hatred of racial discrimination.

Shortly afterwards, he was sent by

his uncle to the jungles of Central India to prospect for iron ore and coal deposits, which were needed to build India's independent steel industry. Although he found the minerals that led to the foundation of Tata Iron and Steel, he fell ill with malaria. As a result he was sent to the health spa at Buxton, in Derbyshire in 1905 to recover.

It was on his birthday, 28th March, that he met his future wife, Sally Marsh and fell in love with her. He proposed to her, on her birthday, and the two were married in 1907. Once a supporter of the Liberal government in Britain, Shapurji Saklatvala began to think that they did not do enough for working people, so he joined the Independent Labour Party (ILP) in 1909. He tried to interest British trade unions in the conditions of workers in India by telling them that their bosses were using India as a

source of cheap labour, so they could pay British workers less. In 1922 he was selected as Parliamentary candidate for Battersea North for the Labour Party. As one newspaper, the Daily Chronicle, said on 8th November 1922: *"Mr Shapurji Saklatvala is a communist...and a sympathiser with the Russian revolution. To do him justice, he makes no secret of these leanings, but rather glories in them. Mr Shapurji Saklatvala will prove too strong even for the Labour element in Battersea."* In fact at the General Election held on 15th November 1922, he won with a comfortable majority. In his first speech in Parliament, Shapurji Saklatvala accused the Government of hypocrisy, because it was working with rulers, such as the Italian fascist dictator, Mussolini and the Serbian King David, who had won power by violence but it would not support the Russian communist government, because they had killed their king, the Tsar.

In 1923, Shapurji Saklatvala lost the election by 186 votes. Now outside Parliament, he went round Britain on speaking tours. In the 1924 General Election, he stood as a Communist candidate and was re-elected. He was the only Communist in the House of Commons and joked that his was the only united party in the House.

During the 1926 General Strike, Shapurji Saklatvala was arrested for making a fiery May Day speech in Hyde Park. He was imprisoned in Wormwood Scrubs for two months. Less than two hours after his release, Shapurji Saklatvala was speaking in Parliament. He explained that he was better off in prison than the miners on strike, because he had been fed and housed, whereas the miners received no money to even buy food for their families.

In early 1927, he went on a speaking tour of India and met Gandhi, but they disagreed over the ways India could win Independence. Shapurji Saklatvala felt that Gandhi's 'simple living' campaign was wrong, saying that furthering progress and increasing living standards for Indian workers was their only hope.

It was his last visit to India, as his visa to enter the country was withdrawn by the British that year. As Shapurji Saklatvala later said, in a speech in Moscow's Red Square, *"I sit in Westminster, making laws for India, and, as an Indian ... I am now told not to go back to my own country."*

He lost his Parliamentary seat in the 1929 General Election, when Labour put up a candidate against him. Soon afterwards he had a heart

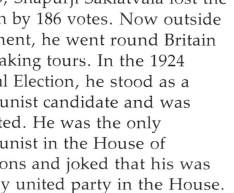

attack. His health failing, he fought two by-elections - Sheffield in 1930 and Battersea in 1931, but was unsuccessful both times.

In 1936 Shapurji Saklatvala died from another heart attack. His memorial tablet at the Zoroastrian Parsi burial ground in Woking reads: *"Nothing but death could end his courage and determination in the cause of humanity. Nothing but such determination could conquer death. His work lives on."*

It would be fifty-eight years before any other non-white MP sat in the House of Commons.

Mrs Bhikhaiji Cama

Bhikhaiji Patel was born in 1861, the same year as Rabindranath Tagore and Motilal Nehru. All three were to have a tremendous impact on the Indian Independence Movement. Tagore inspired a pride in Indian culture with his writings, while Motilal Nehru, father of Jawahalal, the first Prime Minister of India, was the President of the Indian National Congress. Bhikhaiji Cama, the most revolutionary of the three, advocated the use of force to gain Indian Independence.

In 1885, her marriage to the wealthy Rustom Cama was arranged. A different event in the same year proved more significant in her life. The formation of the first Indian National Congress highlighted some of the differences between Bhikhaiji Cama and her new husband. She was already very interested in politics, while he wasn't. After many disagreements, the couple separated, leaving Bhikhaiji Cama to lead her own life.

When plague hit Bombay in 1896,

she became a nurse in a public charity hospital. It was an unheard of action for a wealthy woman and shocked her family and community. At a time when women had few rights and no real prospects outside marriage, she became one of the first Indian women journalists. Her Zoroastrian Parsi community encouraged women to be educated, but even so, Bhikhaiji Cama often scandalised public opinion in the things that she did, such as playing cricket and sometimes wearing Western dress instead of a sari.

Bhikhaiji Cama's tireless work led her to fall ill and she was sent for treatment to Britain in 1902 . After a successful operation, she toured Germany, Scotland and France for several years, finally returning to London. It would be thirty-four years before she went back to India.

In Britain Bhikhaiji Cama met

Dadabhai Naoroji, the first Asian MP in the British Parliament. She helped in his unsuccessful 1906 election campaign and through him, met others working for Indian Independence, including men who had chosen more radical methods than Naoroji. Bhikhaiji Cama agreed with their revolutionary ideas. To raise money for her political activities, she sold the family jewellery her mother had given her to wear in Europe.

Bhikhaiji Cama felt that the use of violence to gain Indian Independence was right. Indians loved peace, she said, but the condition of the Indian people meant that revolution was necessary. Peaceful means, she thought, did not work, so she helped train students in bomb-making and shooting, telling them that, *"Freedom is a conquest and never a bequest"*.

In 1907 she wrote that the British could not imprison the whole Indian population if they refused to co-operate with the British-run government in India. Later that year, Bhikhaiji Cama was invited to speak to the Seventh International Socialist Congress, held in Stuttgart, Germany. At the end of her speech, she unfurled the first design for the Indian national flag to the applause of the audience.

Not surprisingly, Bhikhaiji Cama's activities came to the attention of the British authorities and she was watched by government agents. Secret reports described her thus: *"… she regards herself as engaged in a revolutionary campaign against the British Government in India. She is anarchical, anti-British and irreconcilable."*

To avoid arrest, Bhikhaiji Cama left London to live in France, but the British still asked the French Government to intercept her mail. While in France, she started a revolutionary newspaper.

In the 1920s, Bhikhaiji Cama was involved in a taxi accident, which left her with a broken skull and facial paralysis. Realising that she was gravely ill, and fearing that the British would never allow her back to India, Bhikhaiji Cama chose a grave in Paris. She had a tombstone prepared with the words: RESISTANCE TO TYRANNY IS OBEDIENCE TO GOD carved in both French and Gujarati. The date of her death was given as "192-", the last number to be filled in after her death.

In fact, Bhikhaiji Cama lived in Paris until 1936, when she was finally given permission to return to India. Although Bhikhaiji Cama was by this time barely able to walk or

write, it is a sign of her influence
that she had to promise not to make
any speeches in India before she was
allowed to return to her homeland.
She died in the Parsi General
Hospital in Bombay in August 1936.

Bhikhaiji Cama was an inspiration to
people involved in the
Independence Movement. Her fiery
politics and unstoppable belief in the
right of people to govern themselves
were important to India's eventual
freedom. Today, her portrait hangs
in the Lok Sabha, the Indian
Parliament, as one of the builders of
modern India.

Sir Jagadish Chandra Bose

Sir JC Bose was primarily a scientist. He was honoured by many Western institutions for his innovative research into microwaves and plant behaviour. He was also a man of principle, and fought inequality where he saw it.

After graduating with a Bachelor of Science from St Xavier's College, Calcutta, JC Bose came to England in 1880. He studied natural science at Christ College, Cambridge, and then science at London University. Returning to India in 1885, he took the position of Assistant Professor of Physics at Madras's Presidency College, (founded by Sir Jamsetji Jeejeebhoy).

It was here that he discovered that Indian college lecturers were paid less than British ones. In protest against this injustice, despite severe economic hardship, he refused to draw his pay for three years.

JC Bose's research in the field of electric waves was considered pioneering, and laid the foundations of modern radar. In recognition,

London University conferred a Doctorate of Science on him in 1896. He changed direction soon after this, and between 1899 and 1907, began to study responses from plants and minerals. He was the first person to scientifically prove that plants could feel pain. Between 1908 and 1934 he published many internationally acclaimed scientific papers, defining the borders between life and non-life.

He was knighted in 1916, and retired from the Presidency College in 1917, founding the Bose Institute for Plant Physiological Research two years later. Elected a Fellow of the Royal Society in 1920, he was later to become a Foundation Fellow of the Indian National Science Academy.

When not conducting experiments, JC Bose was interested in many subjects, including philosophy, literature and the arts. His novel in Bengali, *Avykata*, and his detailed

correspondence with Rabindranath Tagore found a wide audience when published. In it, he *"writes memorably of his experiences as a lonely searcher in the world of science"*.

Cornelia Sorabji

Cornelia Sorabji was India's first female professor, Britain's first female law student, and a tireless worker for women's rights. It took her more than twenty years to become a barrister, not because she hadn't completed her studies, but because she was a woman.

She was born a Christian in Nasik, India, in 1866, to parents who had converted to Christianity. Cornelia Sorabji became the first woman student at Poona's Deccan College, gaining a first class degree. This should have won her a state scholarship to study in Britain, but the Indian government insisted that only men could qualify.

At the age of eighteen she became India's first woman professor, teaching English Literature at a college in Ahmedabad, to its all male classes. With the help of her supporters, she eventually raised enough money to continue her studies in Britain.

In 1889, Cornelia Sorabji came to Somerville College, Oxford, to study law. While in Britain, she was introduced to Queen Victoria and some of the people who had given money to enable her to study, including Florence Nightingale.

At that time women were not thought to be clever enough to become lawyers, and Cornelia Sorabji achieved yet another first, being the first woman to study law at any British university.

Although her work was outstanding, she had to overcome many obstacles. Cornelia Sorabji took no notice of the patronising attitudes of her male teachers but soon discovered a more serious problem. She was not allowed to sit the final exams with the three hundred fellow law students, who were all male. She had to get special permission from the Vice Chancellor of Oxford to take the exam paper by herself.

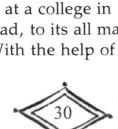

At that time, because of male prejudice, women were not permitted to work as lawyers, either as barristers or solicitors. Cornelia Sorabji was able to join a firm of solicitors as a trainee, but after she returned to India in 1894, despite all her training, it was only with the lower rank of legal adviser.

She spent her life helping women and children, particularly widows, receive practical help from the law. Women in Britain were at last allowed to become barristers in 1919. In 1922 Cornelia Sorabji came back to London, and officially qualified in 1923. She retired six years later and died, aged 88, in 1954.

Cornelia Sorabji had shown that even when women were unable to take their rightful place in the legal and academic world because of society's prejudices, pioneers like herself can use their talents to overcome all odds and help other people to improve their lives.

Krishna Menon (left) with Jawaharlal Nehru

Krishna Menon

Krishna Menon was a Labour councillor in the London Borough of St Pancras before becoming the first Indian High Commissioner to Britain and a leading member of the Indian government after Independence.

Born in Calicut, India, in 1896, even as a child Menon was noted for his abilities to win arguments without a fight. Following in his father's footsteps, he went to Madras' Presidency College, where sons of leading Indians were expected to support British rule. Menon bravely supported Annie Besant's Home Rule League instead. He was nearly expelled for raising the League's flag on the school roof.

In 1924 Menon arrived in London, to study teaching. Although he planned to visit for only six months, he stayed on, studying at the London School of Economics and at University College London, gaining four degrees. By 1934, he had also qualified as a barrister, and fought for justice in cases involving poor Indian sailors, the 'Lascars'.

Menon became the representative of the Indian National Congress in Europe, and in 1934, was elected as a Labour Councillor to the London Borough of St Pancras, (now Camden), where he served for thirteen years. During this time he was responsible for the development of the borough's public library system and started a popular mobile library service. He said, *"I want there to be as many libraries as pubs in the borough."*

He made his living working as a journalist and in 1936 became the editor of the new Pelican paperback books.

Menon was chosen as the Labour candidate for Dundee in 1939, but left the party in 1941, in protest at Labour's opposition to Indian Independence, only rejoining when they changed their policy. By then it was too late for him, because

32

someone else had been selected as Labour's Parliamentary candidate for his old seat.

After Labour's landslide victory in 1945, the movement in Britain towards Indian Independence started. Menon was appointed the Indian representative to the new United Nations in 1946 and 1947, and after Indian Independence in 1947, he became the Indian High Commissioner in London. He led the permanent Indian delegation to the United Nations in 1952, and was elected to the Indian Parliament in 1957, becoming Defence Minister under Prime Minister Nehru.

At the time there was a conflict of ideas between the United States of America and the Soviet Union. Countries like India were asked to align with one side or the other. Menon said, *"If we become aligned, we will be the target of those whom we are not with, and the arsenal of those whom we are with."*

In 1955 he was awarded the freedom of the London Borough of Camden. The only other person given that honour was George Bernard Shaw.

After the Indian election of 1962, he was regarded as the second most powerful person in India after the Prime Minister, Jawaharlal Nehru. When India lost a war with China later that year, he took the blame himself and resigned. After a long retirement from politics, Krishna Menon died in 1974.

Someone once said of him, *"He is no diplomat. He is not even a politician. He is simply an unusually brilliant man."* Throughout the world, Menon's intelligence and integrity helped win respect for his fellow Indians.

Annie Besant (1847-1933) was an Englishwoman. After working in Britain for rights for women, she moved to India, where she tried to win rights for Indians, starting the Home Rule League in 1916. Her work on behalf of the people of India was recognised when the Indian National Congress made her their president, the first woman to be honoured in this way.

Dr Kumar Rupesinghe

Dr Kumar Rupesinghe has spent his life working towards understanding war and conflict, and has been personally responsible for giving the world new ways of thinking about war, how it starts, and what we can do to halt the process.

Born in Sri Lanka, Rupesinghe came to London to study. After receiving a Bachelor of Arts from London University, he returned to Sri Lanka during the 1970s as an advisor to the Prime Minister, Siravamo Bandarananaike, who was the first woman anywhere in the world to head a democratic government.

Rupesinghe edited a popular weekly newspaper while working on a governmental programme that released and rehabilitated more than twenty thousand political prisoners. He was also involved in formulating agriculture reform policy and continued to advise the Prime Minister on a range of issues. When the government was defeated at elections in 1977, Rupesinghe joined the University of Peradeniya and

spent three years lecturing on sociological and development theory.

In 1978, Sri Lanka erupted with political turbulence, and there were violent ethnic clashes between the majority Sinhalese and the minority Tamils. Rupesinghe had been offered an award by the Norwegian Government, which would allow him to study for a Ph.D. in Norway, and he accepted when the situation in Sri Lanka worsened.

In 1982, he was invited to become a research fellow of the International Peace Research Institute in Oslo, (PRIO), and he found himself among a friendly group of Scandinavians who were preoccupied with the global problems of conflict and injustice. While in Oslo, he had the opportunity to reflect on the tragedy of Sri Lanka's recent violence, and became deeply involved with

development, peace and conflict theories.

At the time, theoretical peace research focused almost exclusively on East-West and interstate conflicts. Events in Sri Lanka, as well as visits to Uganda, Lebanon and the Philippines, all areas of violent internal conflicts, convinced Rupesinghe that there was a need for a shift in the way conflict was studied. In 1986, he was offered permanent tenure at PRIO, and had the opportunity to develop further his theories on approaches to ethnic and internal conflicts, and on early warning and preventative diplomacy.

He became Director of PRIO's Programme on Ethnic Conflict and Conflict Resolution. He taught, forged links around the world with other scholars, institutes and with governments, and organised seminars to focus on identifying potential problems and resolving conflicts.

In 1985, he was invited to join the board of International Alert, which had been founded that year by the former Secretary General of Amnesty International, Martin Ennals. International Alert exists to raise international awareness of violent internal conflicts, where there are high risks of massive human rights abuses and even genocide, and where the international community and the parties to the conflict, for whatever reasons, are unaware or unwilling to help sort out the problems. Rupesinghe was appointed Secretary General of International Alert in 1992, which meant a move from Oslo to International Alert's London headquarters. He is also a member of the United Nations University Programme on Internal Conflicts, the Commission on Internal Conflicts and Conflict Resolution,

His work in analysing the theory of peace and conflict has broken new ground, and has meant that, all over the world, there is more of a chance of identifying tensions between peoples and doing something about them, before they turn into wars and massacres.

Noor-un-nisa Inayat Khan

Noor-un-nisa Inayat Khan was a British spy, shot by the Nazis during the Second World War. She was a brave and impetuous woman, who sacrificed her life for her beliefs. Noor's story is an outstanding example of the real impact of the Asian presence in Europe.

Noor was born in 1914, the eldest child of an Indian father and American mother, living in Moscow, Russia. The family had to flee Russia soon afterwards because of the unrest that would lead to the Russian Revolution. They lived in London for six years before settling in Paris. Noor was thirteen when her father, Inayat Khan, died. Her mother became ill, so Noor took over the running of the home and looking after her sister and two brothers.

She studied at Paris University. After graduating in Child Psychology, she began to write children's stories, which were published in France and Britain and performed on radio. A collection of her stories was published in 1939, as *Twenty Jataka Tales Retold*.

In 1939 Hitler's armies began their march across Europe, and conquered nations one by one. Noor and her sister, Khair-un-nisa, trained as nurses to tend wounded French soldiers. Finally, in 1940 when France surrendered to the German Army, the family escaped to London. In Britain, they planned to do all they could to oppose the Nazi regime.

Noor believed strongly in independence and freedom for all the peoples of the world. She realised that if the Indian role in fighting the War was recognised, then a bridge might be built between the British and the Indian peoples that would endure after the War.

At the age of twenty-six, Noor volunteered for the Air Force, where

one of her brothers, Vilyat, was a fighter pilot. He advised her that the way to be recruited was to pick an English sounding name, and to say that she was a Christian. At first she was rejected for not being a British citizen, but after writing a letter complaining about her treatment, she was allowed to join the Women's section of the RAF - the WAAF. Under her adopted name of Nora, she became one of the first women to train as a radio operator.

Noor applied to become an officer in 1942. Her superiors decided that she was not suitable for promotion, when she truthfully admitted that she would support the cause of Indian Independence once the War was over. However, people with language skills were in demand, both for war work in Britain, and as spies in Occupied Europe. It was recognised that, as Noor was bilingual and had lived in Paris, she could be useful as a secret agent.

Even though the head of the organisation was told that she was too impatient, he was impressed by her abilities. The job of radio operator in an occupied country was one of the most dangerous for a spy, because the radio equipment was so bulky and hard to hide. During the war, the BBC often broadcast coded messages to the spies working in Europe, so the Nazis had made listening to the radio an offence for a French citizen.

Noor was offered the chance to stay in the relative safety of London, but even though she knew the dangers, Noor insisted on going to Paris, where she was most needed. Recently engaged to a British officer, she told her friends, *"Everything I've ever wanted has come at once."* Before leaving, her palm was read by a fortune-teller. One of the lines on the hand is said to represent the person's life, and Noor had always noticed that she had a short 'life line'. *"If I have a short life it is because I am reckless,"* she commented.

Finally, it was agreed, it was time for her to return to Paris, and she was given the codename, 'Madeleine'. She was so small physically, (160 cm tall and weighing 49 kg), that a parachute could not be found to fit her, because they were designed for men. So she was flown across the Channel, in a small plane that could set down in a field. This made her mission even more dangerous, as a plane landing was a much more obvious target.

As her French Resistance contact wasn't there to meet her, Noor returned on the plane to England. Her superiors offered her the chance

to stay but Noor turned them down. She returned to France, and this time her contact was waiting.

Noor settled into her double life in Paris, using her quick wit and charm to smooth situations that could have given her away. Surprisingly, she lived in an apartment building that was also home to many German officers. A month after her arrival, the Germans captured some leading members of the French Resistance, including the only other radio operator. Told by London that she could leave, Noor knew that she was the most important radio operator in France, and that her work was crucial to saving lives. She chose to stay.

She was often careless, and other members of her Resistance group would point out that little things, like putting the milk in her tea first, were English habits that could put her in danger, but Noor always forgot to change her behaviour. She was also criticised by fellow agents for leaving secret documents in a room, where anyone could have discovered them.

One day, she was forced to transmit from her flat. A German soldier caught her trying to hang the aerial from a tree in the garden, but Noor charmed him into helping her, and he went off without realising his mistake.

Once questioned by a German soldier who noticed her carrying her radio, Noor glibly told him about her 'film projector', pointing out this 'feature' and that. The soldier was fooled, and soon she was on her way, to a meeting of her Resistance group.

In October, 1943, Noor's luck began to run out. Two Germans pretending to be Canadian had infiltrated her network, and many of the group were trapped. Noor managed to escape Paris, having been told by her superiors to hide in Normandy. Two days later, against orders, she returned to Paris, hoping to continue her work. Realising that her network was broken, she reluctantly agreed to leave France. Before she could escape, she was betrayed, and the Gestapo caught her with her radio and notebooks. Knowing that the penalty for spying was death, Noor asked to be shot immediately. When this was refused, she asked to take a bath. Hoping that she would be helpful if treated well, her captors agreed. Noor made such a fuss over the guards watching her undress that they shut the door, leaving her alone in the bathroom. She promptly climbed out the window, but was recaptured. They offered her easier

conditions if she would stop trying to escape, but she refused. After three more failed attempts, she was placed in chains.

Regarded by the Nazis as highly dangerous, Noor became the first captured British agent to be transported to a proson in Germany. After the Normandy landings in June 1944, the war started to go badly for the Nazis. As they were pushed back across Europe, they retaliated by shooting many captured agents.

On the 11th September, 1944, after ten months in prison, Noor was transported to Dachau concentration camp. The next day, Noor-un-nisa Inayat Khan, along with three other agents, was shot. Her last word in French was *"Liberte!"*, or as we would say *"Freedom!"*

In Britain, her mother and brother both had the same dream. Noor appeared to them in uniform, her happy face surrounded by blue light. *"I'm free,"* she told them.

Noor's work as a spy had helped defeat the Nazis, and although her life had been sacrificed, her bravery was recognised, and Britain's highest civilian award for bravery, the George Cross, was awarded posthumously. The French awarded her the Croix de Guerre (with gold star) for her heroism and self-sacrifice, and erected a monument to her memory.

In Britain, almost every town has a monument to all those who died fighting in the two World Wars. These memorials are inscribed with the line, LEST WE FORGET. We should remember Noor, one of a generation of young people, who fought like tigers for freedom.

> Noor was the great-great-great-granddaughter of the Muslim emperor, Tipu Sultan, who was killed fighting the British in 1799. Known as the Tiger of Mysore, Tipu Sultan was a fierce resister to British rule, saying, *"Better two days as a tiger than two hundred years as a sheep."*

> Inayat Khan, Noor's father, was a famous musician and lived in Paris for several years when he was young. Like most struggling musicians, he worked for a while as part of a backing band, playing for Mata Hari, one of the most famous dancers of the day. During the First World War, (1914-18), she was shot by the French as a German spy.

Professor J E Banatvala

One of the world's leading specialist in diseases caused by viruses, such as the common cold, influenza and AIDS, Jehangir Banatvala was appointed Professor of Clinical Virology at St Thomas's Hospital Medical School, London in 1975. It is a measure of Professor Banatvala's output that at one period, he had sixteen research papers and books awaiting release to join hundreds of earlier publications.

He was born in Kilburn, London in 1934 to parents who had emigrated from Bombay at the time of the Great Depression. Having finished a course at the London School of Hygiene and Tropical Medicine, Professor Banatvala was looking for *"something glamorous in the **World Health Organisation**"*, when a virology research post came up at Cambridge. Not liking laboratory work, but liking Cambridge, he took the post.

Professor Banatvala is due to retire around the year 2000 and plans to relax and do some of the things he has not had time for. He asks that people should not *"get hooked to their past ethnic origins. It is likely to upset your children and my parent's views drove me up the wall!"*

Now as Head of Department at one of London's most prestigious teaching hospitals, when asked if there was any advice he would like to give to a younger generation, he at first said, *"I do not feel I should be so presumptuous."* He did add that if a young person had two options they should pick the more exciting one and that enjoyment of life and work was most important.

Prince Ranjitsinhji

Prince Ranjitsinhji and C B Fry

Prince Ranjitshinhji, heir to the throne of the Jam Saheb of Nawanagar, played cricket for England at the turn of the century, and captained Sussex.

India's cricket history is almost as long as England's, with the Calcutta Cricket Club founded in 1792, not long after the start of the Marylebone Cricket Club, (better known as the M.C.C.), in England. The first Indian cricket tour of England was in 1886.

Prince Ranjitsinhji was born in 1872 and came to Britain in 1888. Two years later, he became a student at Cambridge, where he was nicknamed 'Smith', impressing everyone with his batting skill. Joining Sussex County Cricket Club after leaving Cambridge, he captained the side for five years and scored over a thousand runs in each of his twelve full seasons, despite suffering from hay-fever throughout the summer.

When Australia came to England to play a test series in 1896, Prince Ranjitsinhji was called up for the second test in Manchester. Although he failed to prevent Australia winning, his scores of 62 and 154 not out made him the best English batsman of the day. Called 'Run Getsinhji' by the magazine Punch, he was also selected for a tour of Australia.

On his retirement from cricket, he served on the League of Nations, where a former colleague at Sussex County Cricket Club was the British representative. Prince Ranjitsinhji died in 1933.

Jahangir Khan

Jahangir Khan became the youngest ever World Champion squash player, and one of the greatest, winning over 500 matches in a row. He says, *"I believe my story can offer hope to millions of people all over the world who are poor, bereaved or sick. At different times, I have been all three..."*

Born in Pakistan in 1964, the young Jahangir was often ill, and was told not to play squash. In spite of this, when no-one was around, he would practise against a wall. When Jahangir was finally allowed to play squash, after finishing his homework each day, he won the Pakistan Junior Title and a place on the Pakistan Junior Team.

At that time his elder brother, Torsam, ranked second in the world, was living in Britain. As Britain had the coaching facilities and opportunities for match experience that Jahangir needed, Torsam asked Jahangir to join him. However while playing in a tournament in Australia, Torsam died after a heart attack. Jahangir returned to Pakistan for the funeral.

Success in squash was taken very seriously in Pakistan, and Jahangir realised that he now had a duty to become the world's best squash player. He was offered a large house with servants, but decided to return to Britain to train for the World Championships.

At that time the world champion was the Australian, Geoff Hunt. Even though Jahangir was in mourning and homesick, and finding the English climate and language strange, he started a rigorous training programme, and *"would usually be too tired to be unhappy"*.

Jahangir and Hunt faced each other in the 1981 British Open final. This time Hunt's experience gave him victory. Jahangir now aimed to win the 1981 World Championships, but

had an injured arm and thought that he would not be able to play. He decided however to compete especially sine the final was to be played on 28th November, the anniversary of Torsam's death. Winning the World Championship at the age of just seventeen, Jahangir knelt on the Toronto court in prayer, to give thanks for his victory and in memory of his brother.

During the 1980's, Jahangir became unbeatable, creating new records, in the number of world championships and British Open wins, which will be difficult to beat for many years to come.

His advice to those who wish to follow his success is simple: *"Don't follow the rest of the world, the rest of the world doesn't want to become World Champion"*.

Rabindranath Tagore

Rabindranath Tagore took traditional Indian literature into the twentieth century, reaching a world-wide audience in the process. For many great poems, plays and novels, he was awarded the Nobel Prize for Literature in 1913.

Born in Calcutta in 1861, into a famous Bengali family, Tagore did not go to school as often as he should have done. When he managed to come first in the Bengali examination, a teacher said, *"It can't be, he hasn't been at school often enough. He has been given high marks because he is from a wealthy family."* So Tagore was made to retake the exam, this time in the presence of an inspector, and again came first.

Even at the age of ten, the quality of his poetry was so mature and sophisticated, that people found it hard to believe that such a young boy had written it. In fact several of his fellow pupils accused him of copying the lines from a book, but he decided to let them think what they liked.

In 1875 aged fourteen, Tagore was appointed the official poet of a young people's secret society, the *Hanchu Pamu Haph*, whose aim was to end British rule.

In 1878, when seventeen, he was sent to study in Britain. He spent a short time in a school in Brighton, where he was treated as a novelty by the other boys.

Moving to London, Tagore stayed with the family of a Mr Scott. The family's two daughters ran away, fearing the strange Indian youth, but soon returned on being told of his 'English' qualities. Writing later, Tagore said, *"One thing struck me when living with this family that human nature is everywhere the same."*

He studied at the University of London, and on returning to India, composed and starred in his first musical drama *Valmiki Pratibha*, or

44

The Genius of Valmiki.

It wasn't till 1890, when Tagore was put in charge of the family's land, that he learned anything about the lives of the ordinary Indian people. On asking a servant why he was late for work, the man replied that he was returning from the grave of his eight year old daughter. Tagore was touched by the death of someone so young, and, as a result, began to write stories about Indian village life, showing that if people worked together to look after themselves, they could achieve more.

The English language was used at political meetings, but Tagore said that Bengalis should be proud of their own language. He was also angry about the gap between the rich people and ordinary folk, and wrote poems that criticised the *"pleasure seekers"* and their *"hankering after fame"*.

In 1911, he became ill and was told to go to Britain for treatment. The trip was postponed however when he had a serious fall. While he was recovering he translated his Bengali works into English, and only left India later that year.

While travelling on the London Underground, he left all his precious poems on the train. Luckily, they were recovered. Tagore had his poetry printed in English, and *Gitanjali*, or *Song Offerings* was published in 1912. Tagore won the Nobel Prize for Literature in 1913, the first Indian to have done so.

He began his great university of Indian culture, Visva Bharati, in 1919, saying it, *"was where the world comes together in a single nest"*. Two years later, he dedicated the university to India and in order to raise funds for it, he gave it the copyright of all his writings. In 1936 his great friend, Gandhi, appealed for money for the university rather than see Tagore, by then aged seventy-five, have to beg for funds himself.

He died in Calcutta in 1941. The author of over three thousand poems and two thousand songs, as well as eight novels and fifty plays, Rabindranath Tagore had influenced generations of Indians to take pride in their culture and heritage. In a fitting tribute, one of his poems was adapted as the words for the Indian National Anthem.

Uday Shankar and Anna Pavlova

Uday Shankar

Along with his brother Ravi, Uday Shankar brought the arts of India to the attention of the worlds of dance and music. He was the first modern Indian dancer, and though untrained, was to dance on the world's stages for fifty years.

Uday Shankar was born in Udaipur, India, in 1900. He went to the Sir Jamsetji Jeejeebhoy School of Art, India's most famous art college, then attended the Royal College of Art, in London. While studying painting, he appeared in variety shows as a magician, and also performed as a dancer. He was about to leave London, to take part in an art competition in Rome, when he was asked to meet Anna Pavlova, the famous Russian ballerina.

Ann Pavlova, who wanted an Indian dancer, asked him to work with her troupe. When he saw her, he changed his mind about Rome, and agreed to choreograph two dances for her, dancing in one of them himself. Uday Shankar's teachers were furious, but Pavlova told them,

"God never gives such bodies to painters and sculptors: they do not need them".

Since he was not a trained Indian dancer, Uday Shankar's work was very different from the traditional Indian styles. His dances were chosen for their expressive quality. The troupe toured the world, and in America, reviewers praised Uday Shankar's work as *"mystical, tender and of an indescribable grace and movement."*

In 1929, he left Pavlova's company and returned to India, where he started a company of Indian dancers and musicians who would tour the West. The whole family, including his ten year old brother, Ravi, moved to France to join him in the successful new company.

In 1940, he closed the company and moved back to India to start a Cultural Centre, but after four years

he was forced to close it, as the money had run out. He then made a film, *Kalpana*, which, although an artistic triumph, was a commercial flop. When it failed to make money, Uday Shankar went back to his world tours from 1949 until 1968.

Most dancers stop performing in their mid-thirties, but Uday Shankar was now twice that age and gradually began to give his parts to others to perform. The 1968 American tour was cut short when he had a stroke. His artistic invention continued however, as the director and producer of Shankarscope. Today it would be called performance art, a combination of cinema and live dance. Some dancers would be seen on the screen at one moment, then 'magically' appear live on stage, while others repeated the movements of giant figures on the screen. After more ill health however, he eventually retired, very unhappy, frail and sick.

It had seemed to him that the people of India had forgotten him, but when he died in Calcutta in 1977, the news made headlines in India and, as a mark of respect, government offices were closed for a day.

Uday Shankar is remembered today as a great innovator, and as the first contemporary Indian dancer.

Shobana Jeyasingh

Shobana Jeyasingh is an exciting choreographer and artistic director, working in Asian and European contemporary dance, and directing her own dance company.

Shobana was born in Madras, India and now lives in London. Her work for theatre and television performance has won many awards, including a London Dance and Performance Award in 1988, and in 1992, she became three times winner of the Digital Dance Award. In 1993, the Arts Council of Great Britain, through their Women in the Arts Project, made an award which acknowledged her valuable contribution to the arts in the past decade.

She has produced radical works like *Duets with Automobiles*, a short film, and choreographed Shakespeare's *Twelfth Night*, for the Theatre Royal in Stratford East. She worked on *The Little Clay Cart* with Jatinder Verma in 1991 and 1992, which was performed at the prestigious National Theatre. In 1993, her company was the overall winner of the Prudential Award for the Arts, one of the United Kingdom's most prestigious awards.

Shobana herself was awarded an MBE, and is invited to choreograph new work all over the world.

Darshan Singh Bhuller

Darshan Singh Bhuller in the ballet *Petrushka*

Darshan Singh Bhuller's dancing has been described as *"electrifying"*, and *"so ethereal ... almost godly"*. He says he is not a ballet dancer, and that cinema, the first form of theatre he saw, has been a great influence.

Darshan was born in Singapore in 1961. Shortly afterwards his Punjabi Sikh family moved to the Punjab for seven years, before coming to Britain. They lived in Chapeltown in Leeds, where Darshan's father worked on a building site. It was by chance, while at his local school, that he started to dance. As part of a state initiative to promote the arts, all the pupils became very involved in dance and drama.

After leaving school, Darshan and many of his classmates stayed in the arts. In 1980 he joined the London Contemporary Dance Theatre, where his distinctive stage presence led to choreographer, Richard Alston, creating dances especially for him. He won an Olivier Award in 1994. The same year, the LCDT closed, due to funding cuts. This led Darshan to join Richard Alston's new Dance Company, based at the Place Theatre in London, where he continues to dance, choreograph and teach his special art form.

Darshan has already directed a short film, *The Fall*, about a dancer confined to a wheelchair, which was shown on Channel Four, and nominated for a British Film Institute award. Darshan says, in the future, he would like to do more directing and one day run his own dance company.

As he was growing up, being a ballet dancer never crossed his mind, and even now, he considers himself to be doing exactly what he wants to do: contemporary art. When asked about the image breaking nature of his work, Darshan replied that at sixteen, he simply did what came naturally, and didn't realise he was being iconoclastic in his choices. He says that young people should do what

they feel is "it", whatever "it" is for them. Finally, Darshan says the best choices are made simply by going with the flow of life.

Robin Dutt

Robin Dutt is a journalist and a pioneer in the world of style and design.

Born in Notting Hill Gate, London, his family has a long history in Great Britain. His great-grandfather, the poet, Manmohan Ghose, along with his two brothers, Barindro and Aurobindo, came to study in England in the nineteenth century. After St Pauls School and Oxford, Manmohan became friends with Oscar Wilde, W B Yeats, and Walter de la Mare, who heralded him as the flower of Indian poetry. Barindro became an Indian freedom fighter and died for his political beliefs in Port Blair, Andaman Islands, which was then a prison. The most famous of the brothers was Sri Aurobindo, the world-renowned philosopher and thinker.

As a boy, Robin felt unable to fulfil his dream of becoming a poet. However after seeing the rock-musical, *The Rocky Horror Show*, he was struck by the advice of the hero, *"Don't dream it, be it!"*, and decided to channel his energies and talents into creative writing. His interests in fine art and style led him to write articles on interiors. As a journalist, he has written for many foreign newspapers and magazines, and was the menswear correspondent for BBC Television's *Clothes Show Magazine*. He has also broadcast on BBC Radio's *World Service*.

Robin now works with his colleague, Sarah Millar, staging exhibitions at the West Soho Gallery in London, to further the appreciation of contemporary artists. As part of his vision, he seeks out talent, wherever it may be, and gives it a stage.

by a gang of white racists on a young British Asian in Tower Hamlets, London in 1993. But he did not stop there. He met the young people and donated money from the sales of *Movin On* to them.

In his Birmingham office, Apache Indian has a plaque above his desk which reads: PEOPLE WILL DOUBT WHAT YOU SAY BUT THEY WILL ALWAYS BELIEVE WHAT YOU DO.

Apache Indian is using the power of his music and fame to fight prejudice and to break down barriers between people.

GLOSSARY

Align: A country especially friendly with another country or a group of countries, is said to be aligned with them.

Assassination: The killing of a leader.

Aviator: A person who can fly an aeroplane, from the name of the science of flight, aviation.

Barrister: A lawyer trained to argue a case in court.

Bilingual: A person able to speak two languages fluently.

Brahmin: The caste system is a way of dividing people into a series of groups. In India, each caste has a different set of rules saying what they can and cannot do and each caste is dependent on the others. Brahmins are the caste that include priests and educators.

Brahmo Samaj: Started in the 18th Century as a social reform movement but later became a religious movement.

Campaign: An organised attempt to change something.

Campaigner: A person who starts or organises a campaign.

Choreographer: A person who designs/arranges ballet or stage dance.

Collaboration: Working jointly especially at literary or artistic productions.

Concentration Camp: A prison for civilians held because of their beliefs or nationality. The most infamous camps were those of Nazi Germany.

Concerto: Composition for an orchestra and one or more soloists.

Conductor: The leader or guide of an orchestra who indicates rhythm by gestures.

Constituency: The area represented by a Member of Parliament.

Contemporary: Belonging to the same time; modern.

Debut: First appearance on stage or in sport as a performer.

Democracy: Where most or all of the population takes some part in running a country usually by voting for people to represent their views. From the Greek words for 'people' and 'rule'.

Dictator: A ruler who has total control of his people.

Doctorate: A very advanced qualification.

East India Company: A British private company which was granted a charter by Queen Elizabeth I on 31st December 1600 to trade in the East Indies - Asia. It became involved in politics in the early 18th Century and was very powerful as it was given the right to coin its own money, raise its own armies in India and even make war against non-Christian countries. Following the Indian Mutiny in 1857, power was transferred to the British government and India came under the direct rule of the British crown.

EC: The European Community.

Economics: The study of how people produce, sell, buy and use things.

Election/By-election: A way of choosing someone by voting. The person with the largest number of votes is chosen. If the person elected dies or retires, a by-election is needed to choose someone to replace them.

Emancipation: Freeing from social, legal, political or moral restrictions.

Exemplifies: To show by example.

Forerunner: Someone or something that goes before.

French Resistance: An illegal organisation of French people fighting for freedom against Nazi occupation of France during World War II.

Genocide: Deliberate killing of a race of people.

Great Depression: A world-wide economic depression of the early 1930s, when there was great unemployment.

Heritage: Anything that passes from one generation to another or is handed down by tradition.

High Commissioner: the senior diplomat sent by one Commonwealth

GLOSSARY

country to another instead of an ambassador.

Hindu: A person believing in Hinduism, which is the main religion of India. Hindus believe in many gods, the caste system, reincarnation (people being reborn after death in a different form) and the importance of doing good in this life, so that the next life will be better.

Home Rule League: Started by Annie Besant in 1916, the league campaigned for Indian Independence, known at the time as 'Home Rule'.

Hypocrisy: Pretending to good or virtuous.

Iconoclast: A person who attacks established or traditional concepts/views.

Independence: being able to make political decisions. For many years before Indian Independence, most decisions affecting India were made by the British.

Indian National Congress: From small beginnings in December 1885, the Indian National Congress became the main place for Indians to discuss their ideas for India's future. At first, it met every year and its few members wanted India to stay under British rule. Later, it had millions of members who worked for Indian Independence.

Industrialist: A person who has the ownership or control of a major industrial company/organisation.

Infiltrate: To go through enemy held lines or positions without being caught or noticed.

Innovator: A person who makes something new or brings in changes.

Journalist: A person who writes for a newspaper or the media.

Lascar: An Indian word for 'sailor'. It is still used to describe any Indian sailor.

Magistrate: A person administrating laws.

Marxist: Someone/something which supports the beliefs of *Karl Marx* (1818-1883) a philosopher and economist. His works are used as the basis of the economic system called Communism.

Memorial tablet: A stone or structure that marks a grave.

Migrant: Someone who moves from place to place.

Muslim: A member of the Islamic faith. Muslims are expected to obey Allah's wishes completely, praying several times a day.

Nazi: A person who is a member of the Nationalist Socialist Workers Party which gained control of Germany in 1933 under *Adolf Hitler*. The party used violent ways to make the people of their country do what they wanted.

Parliament: The group of people who make laws for a country. The Parliament for the UK consists of the Queen, the House of Lords and the House of Commons.

Parsi: After Persia (the old name for Iran) was conquered by Muslims, most of Persia's Zoroastrians became Muslims. Some fled, eventually arriving in India. There they were known as Parsis, 'people from Persia'. Over a thousand years later, the name is still used to describe Zoroastrians in India.

Partition: 'Division'. When India won Independence, many Muslims wanted to live in a country of their own. So the main sub-continent was divided into different countries: India, East and West Pakistan (East Pakistan is now Bangladesh) and Ceylon (now Sri Lanka). This was known as the Partition of India.

PhD: Doctor of philosophy

Philanthropist: A person who loves mankind and carries out good acts.

Philosopher: A person who thinks and writes about knowledge and ideas.

Pioneer: A person who takes the lead in a particular action and is followed later

GLOSSARY

by others.

Psychology: The science of the nature and function of the mind.

Racial Discrimination: Judging people on their race rather than on their abilities or character.

Radical: A person who wants to see major changes.

Raga: A complete melody based on a specific tune.

Raja/Rajah: An Indian prince/nobleman.

Reforms: Changes, hopefully for the better.

Regime: A system of government or laws.

Revolution: The violent overthrow of a government.

Revolutionary: A person who wants to change things by force, not through elections.

Rupee: Indian currency.

Sloop: A small one-masted ship.

Sociology: The science of human development, behaviour and laws.

Suffragette: A woman who fights to give women the right to vote in political elections.

Troupe: A company of actors/performers.

Visa: An official approval in a passport which allows the holder of the passport to enter or leave a country.

WAAF: (Women's Auxiliary Air Force) When Noor-un-nisa Khan's brother joined Britain's Royal Air Force, she was only allowed to join the WAAF. Members of WAAF wore a uniform but were not allowed to fight.

Zoroastrian: A person who is a member of the first religion to teach that there is only one god, founded by Zarathustra around 3500 years ago. The basic commandment to Zoroastrians is to speak good works, think good thoughts and do good deeds.

Other non-fiction titles from **Mantra**:

Exploring Series:
Scripts of the World
Indian Food
Caribbean Food
Chinese Food
Indian Crafts
Islamic Arts

Makers of History Series:
Dadabhai Naoroji
Mandela, Time to be Free
Indian Women of our Time

Educational Project Packs:
Fruit
Mathematics Around the World
Water